How to Make and fly kites

How to

Make and fly kites

Eve Barwell and
Conrad Bailey

STUDIO VISTA London

VNR **VAN NOSTRAND REINHOLD COMPANY** New York

Acknowledgments

The authors would like to thank all those friends, amongst them Gary (whose photograph appears on page 52) and Denise Wingrove, who helped test fly the kites in this book.

A Studio Vista/Van Nostrand Reinhold How-to Book

Text and drawings copyright © 1972 by Eve Barwell and Conrad Bailey
Photographs copyright © 1972 by Studio Vista
Photoset, printed and bound in England by
BAS Printers Limited, Wallop, Hampshire
Published in Great Britain by
Studio Vista
Blue Star House, Highgate Hill, London N19
and in the United States by
Van Nostrand Reinhold Company
A Division of Litton Educational Publishing, Inc.
450 West 33rd Street, New York, NY 10001
Library of Congress Catalog Card Number 79–161974

ISBN 0 289 70228 3

Contents

How to use this book

Read the opening section (pages 8–15) very carefully. This is the most important part of the book. It suggests which materials to use and explains the six main steps in kitemaking.

Decide which kite to make first and follow the numbered instructions for it. At the same time keep turning back to the opening section of the book for help with the six main stages.

Read the last section (pages 60–67) when your kite is finished. It will help you to fly it really well.
If you have never made or flown a kite before, start by making one of the easier kites. These are the Bat, Box 2, Cutter and Fish.

How to choose your materials

Most of the materials used to make the kites in this book may be found around the house. Choose covers and sticks that weigh as little as possible. The lighter the kite, the better it will fly.

Covers
Most kites have a cloth or paper cover but you can experiment with other materials. Whatever you choose, the wind must not be able to blow through it. Suitable materials are:

paper: brown paper
crêpe paper
fancy wrapping paper
imitation Japanese paper (from a shop
   selling artists' materials)
newspaper
shelf paper
tissue paper
wallpaper

fabric: artificial silk
closely woven cotton
lining materials
silk

oddments: coloured plastic sacks
plastic wrapping materials
(polythene, Saran Wrap, etc.)
polystyrene tiles

Glue
Evo-stik will stick most of the materials mentioned in this book.

If you are making a polystyrene kite, test your glue on it first. Some glues 'melt' polystyrene and it is best to use the recommended tile cement.

For sticking plastics, polythene and Saran Wrap it is quicker and easier to use Sellotape, Scotch tape, or a similar adhesive tape.

Sticks
Each stick must be evenly balanced as well as light. To test one, mark the centre of the stick and balance it across a pencil held in your hand. If one end hangs lower than the other, shave a little of it away with a knife.

Suitable materials are:
balsa wood (from a crafts and hobbies shop)
batons or dowelling
bamboo canes (from a gardening shop. Split them lengthwise with a knife to make them lighter.)
garden sticks (gardening shop)
old umbrella spokes
sticks from trees and hedges

String or cord
Any thin string or nylon or terylene cord may be used for making kites.

Six steps in kitemaking

How to bind and glue the sticks

Wherever two or more sticks cross they must be tied and glued together. This gives the kite a really firm framework.

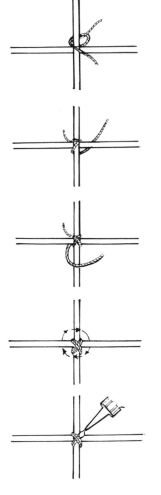

Lay the sticks in position. Tie on a piece of string or cord.

Wind the cord round the join like this . . .

. . . then like this.

And then weave it round, over and under the sticks like this.

Cover the cord with dabs of glue. Leave it to dry.

How to frame the kite

Most kites need a frame of string or cord. It helps the kite keep its shape and makes a firm edge for the cover.

Cut a notch in the end of each stick like this.

Tie a piece of string to one of the sticks. Leave a fairly long end.

Keeping the string taut, take it across to the notch on the next stick and wind it round two or three times.

Wind the string round all the sticks in turn until you are back where you started. Tie the two ends of the string together.

(For a cutter kite, cut the notches like this. Simply slot the string into the notches and pull it tight before you knot the two ends together.)

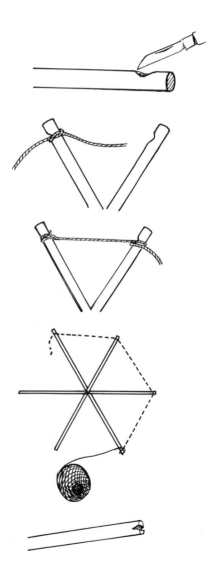

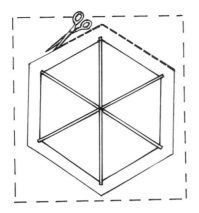

How to cover the kite

Lay the framework on the material you have chosen for the cover. Cut round it, cutting the cover larger than the frame all the way round.

Cut away the corners of the cover.

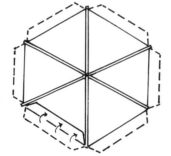

Bend the edges of the cover over the frame and stick them down with glue or adhesive tape.

Cut little notches in any curved edges of the cover before gluing them down.

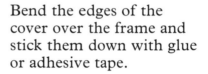

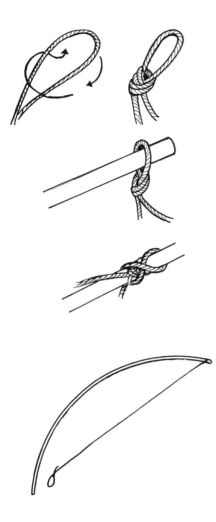

How to bow the kite

Many kites will fly better if they have a curved or bowed surface towards the wind instead of a flat one.

Cut a piece of string 15 cm (6 in.) longer than the stick you want to bow. Bend each end back 7·5 cm (3 in.) and knot them like this.★

Lay the kite face down and slip one of the loops over one end of the stick.

Stop the loop slipping along the stick by winding string round it in a figure eight.

Bend the stick gently until you can slip the other loop over the other end. Fasten it in position in the same way.

★ These measurements are a useful guide for a medium-sized kite. For very large kites the string will have to be shorter than this (perhaps the same length as the stick) and for very small kites it will have to be longer.

How to make the bridle
The short strings from the ends of the sticks to the towing ring are called the bridle. They hold the kite at the correct angle to the wind while it is flying. A curtain ring makes a good towing ring.

Tie a piece of cord or string to the top of the spine. (The spine is the stick that goes from top to bottom of the kite.) The instructions for the individual kite will tell you how long that string should be.

Loop it two or three times through a curtain ring and tie it to the bottom of the spine. Slide the ring along the string until it is in the right place. (It will always be nearer the top of the kite than the bottom.)

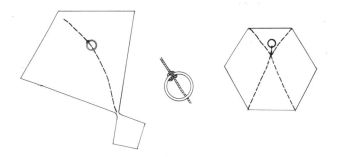

Some kites have a double bridle. This means they have another string tied to each end of one of the other sticks. This piece of string is looped through the curtain ring too.

When the ring is in the right position on the strings, wind a small piece of adhesive tape round the strings behind the ring to hold it firm.

How to make a tail

Box kites do not need a tail. Almost every other kind of kite does. Some need more than one. Often a tail has to be up to five times as long as the kite so as to help it balance properly. Make the tail from the same material as the kite.

Cut your paper, fabric or plastic into strips about 20 cm (8 in.) by 5 cm (2 in.). Tie the strips onto a long piece of string, spacing them about 20 cm (8 in.) apart. It will help if you anchor one end of the string to a door handle or chair leg before you start. Tie the finished tail to the bottom of the kite.

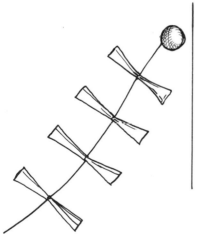

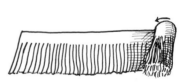

If your kite is small and very light you will need a very light tail. Try a paper tassel. Cut a long narrow strip of paper about 50 cm (20 in.) long and 10 cm (4 in.) wide. Cut a deep fringe in one of the long edges, then roll the paper up tightly. Bind the top with adhesive tape. Use a piece of string about the same length as the kite to tie the tassel to it.

15

Kites
Aero-kite

You need:
2 sticks the same length
1 stick about one third as long as the others
paper
string and curtain ring
glue, pencil and ruler

1 Use the pencil to mark the centre of each of the three sticks. Divide one of the longer sticks in half again. Lay out the three sticks as in the diagram. Bind and glue them were they touch (see page 10).

2 Frame the sticks (see page 11), crossing the frame cords at point **a**.

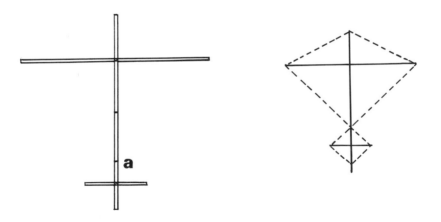

3 Cover the frame (see page 12). Snip the cover each side of point **a** so that the cover may be folded and glued down more easily.

4 Bow the wings and tail (see page 13).

Bridle (see page 14). Cut a piece of string a little longer than the wing section of the plane. Tie it to the top of the kite and point **a**.

Tail. This kite should fly without a tail.

Decoration. Paint the insignia of the air force or the initials of an airline onto the wings of the plane.

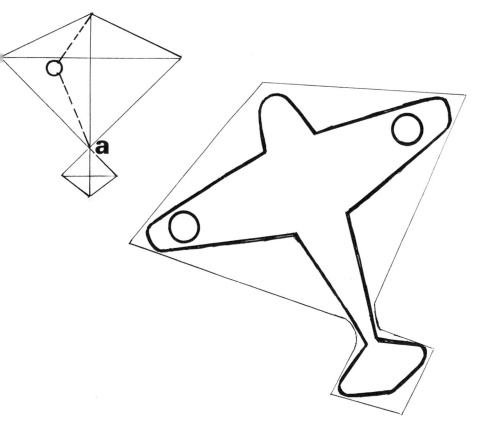

Balloon kite

You need:
a large polystyrene tile (from a paint and wallpaper shop)
an old kitchen knife
a candle
two long sticks
string, curtain ring
glue (see page 9!)
pencil, ruler, paints
balloons

1 Using the ruler and pencil draw your kite on the tile like this:

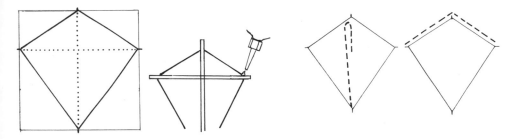

2 Heat the blade of the knife over a candle flame for a few seconds and then start to cut out the shape. Whenever the tile becomes difficult to cut, re-heat the knife for another few seconds. *Do this in a well-aired room.*

3 Glue the sticks across the kite from corner to corner, letting them jut out a little at each end. Turn the kite over and leave it to dry.

Bridles (see page 14). Cut a piece of string long enough to reach from top to bottom of the kite and one third of the way back again. Tie it to the top and bottom of the kite. Remember to thread the curtain ring onto it. Cut

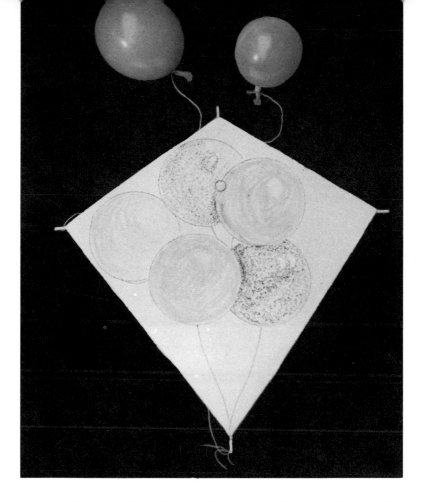

a second piece of string the length of the two short sides of the kite and attach it at each side.

Tail (see page 15). Make a tail about five times the length of the kite and tie it to the bottom stick.

Decoration. Mix a little household emulsion paint with your powder or poster colours and paint some balloons onto the kite. Test the kite to make sure it flies well. Then blow up some real balloons and attach them on strings to the sides and bottom of the kite. Put an equal number on each side.

Bat

You need:
2 sticks the same length
a sheet of polythene, Saran
   Wrap or similar
   (large polythene bag)
glue, adhesive tape
black paper or felt-tipped
   pen
string and curtain ring
ruler and pencil
scissors

1 Mark the exact centre of each stick. Divide one half of one of the sticks into two equal sections. Break off one of these sections and lay one stick across the other as shown in the diagram.

2 Bind and glue the sticks together (see page 10).

3 Lay the sticks on the polythene and use them as a guide for cutting the semi-circular shape. Fix the end of each stick to the polythene with a piece of adhesive tape.

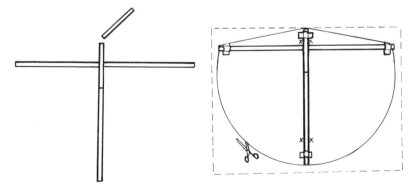

4 Bow the longer stick slightly (see page 13).

Bridle (see page 14). Cut a piece of string a little longer than the centre stick. With the point of your pencil make small holes in the polythene at the points marked ×. You will then be able to thread the string through the cover and tie it to the stick. The curtain ring should be about one quarter of the way along the string.

Decoration. Draw a bat on the polythene with a felt-tipped pen. (You may find it easier to draw the bat shape on thin black paper, cut it out, and stick it to the poly-thene with adhesive tape.

This kite does not need a tail. Try flying it when it is getting dark. The Bat looks really eerie and sounds quite frightening as the polythene flaps in the wind.

Bluebird

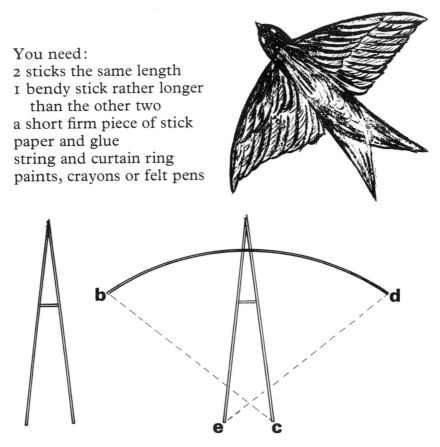

You need:
2 sticks the same length
1 bendy stick rather longer
    than the other two
a short firm piece of stick
paper and glue
string and curtain ring
paints, crayons or felt pens

1 Lay out the two identical sticks and the short firm piece in the shape of an 'A'. Bind and glue the sticks together where they touch (see page 10).

2 Lay the last stick across the A and bind and glue it in position.

3 Attach a string to point **b** and tie the other end to point **c** so that the cross stick is bent. Tie another string from **d** to **e**. Make sure that each wing is bent the same amount.

4 Cover the frame with paper (see page 12).

Bridles. Cut one piece of string to reach from **c** to **x** and back to **e**. Tie the ends to points **c** and **e**, looping the string through the curtain ring as you do so. Cut a second piece of string to reach from **c** to **x** and tie it to the tops of the wings at the points marked **y**, again remembering to loop it through the ring.

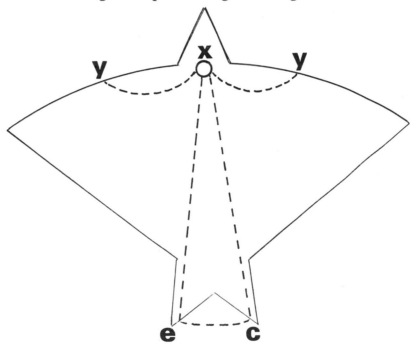

Tail (see page 15). Make a tail about three times the length of the kite. Tie a loop of string from **c** to **e** and hang the tail from it.

Decoration. Paint or draw the feathers onto your Bluebird.

Box kite 1

(colour photograph page 51)
You need:
8 medium sized polystyrene tiles (1 ft. square is ideal)
4 sticks the same length (they should be three times as
   long as one tile)
glue (see page 9!)
adhesive tape
string and curtain ring

1 Lay out four tiles side by side, their edges almost touching, and face down so that you cannot see their slanted edges. Stick adhesive tape all the way along the two long edges.

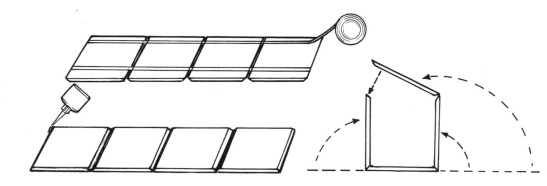

2 Turn the tiles over and spread glue down the slanted edges, as shown in the diagram. Fold the strip of tiles into a box shape and fasten the last corner with tape.

3 Make a second box in exactly the same way.

4 Glue the sticks inside the corners of the boxes, leaving small pieces jutting out at each end. Use adhesive tape to fasten the sticks even more firmly at the top and bottom edges of the boxes (see centre diagram).

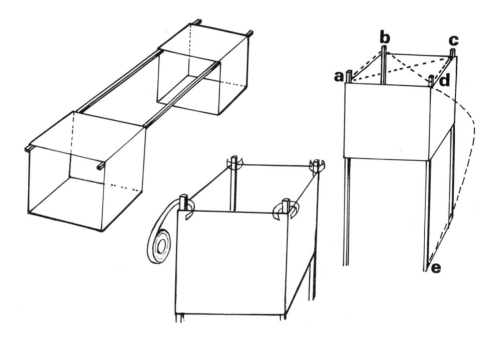

5 Wind string tightly round the sticks to stop the boxes blowing out of shape. To do this, tie the string to **a**, wind it first round **c**, then **d**, then **b**, and back to **a**. Fasten it off firmly.

Repeat this at the other end of the kite.

Bridle. Cut a piece of string four times the length of one tile. Loop the curtain ring onto the string. It should come one quarter of the way along it. Tie the shorter end to point **d** and the longer one to point **e** (see diagram page 25).

Decoration. Give your kite stripes made of coloured sticky tape or glue on a design of coloured paper. If you would rather paint it, mix a little household emulsion paint with your powder or poster paints.

Box kite 2 (triangular)

(colour photograph page 51)
You need:
6 polystyrene tiles
3 sticks three times as long as one tile
string and curtain ring
glue (see page 9!)
adhesive tape

1 Lay out three tiles side by side, leaving small gaps between them. Tape and glue them together as for Box Kite 1. Fold them into a triangle.

2 Make a second triangle in the same way.

3 Finish the kite as for Box Kite 1, ignoring paragraph 5.

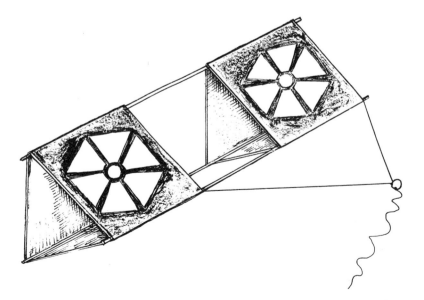

Box kite 3 (cloth)

You need:
7 sticks the same length
light, closely woven fabric
needle and thread (or stapler)
string and curtain ring
pencil and ruler

1 With a pencil divide all seven sticks into three equal sections. Take three of the sticks and break or cut them on the pencil marks.

2 Lay out four of these broken pieces to form a square. Bind and glue them together (see page 10) at the corners. Do the same with another four pieces.

3 Bind and glue the four long sticks to the square frames as shown in the diagram.

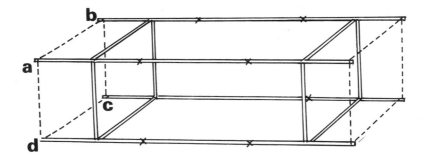

4 Tie a piece of string to point **a**. Pull it tightly across to **b**. Wind it round **b** two or three times, then round **c** and **d** before taking it back to **a** and fastening it off firmly. Make a second string frame at the other end of the kite.

5 Make two more string frames on the pencil marks near the centre of the kite.

6 Cut two strips of fabric. They should be a little wider than the distance between two of the string frames and a little longer than the distance all round one of the frames.

7 Wrap one of the fabric strips round one end of the framework. Pin the two ends together, pulling the fabric tight. Sew along the join and remove the pins.

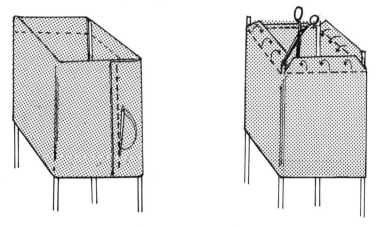

8 Fold the sides of the fabric strip over the string frame. To make this easier, snip the fabric at the corners. Sew these folded edges in position (or clip them down using a small stationery stapler).

9 Cover the other end of the kite in the same way to make the second box.

Bridle. Follow the instructions for Box Kite 1 on page 25.

Butterfly 1

You need:
a large sheet of white paper
coloured tissue paper
3 sticks the same length (two that bend easily and one
   fairly firm)
string
glue
pencil

1 Make two bows with the bendy sticks and string (see page 13). Lay them together to make a butterfly shape that is wider at the top than at the bottom. Bind and glue the sticks where they touch (see page 10).

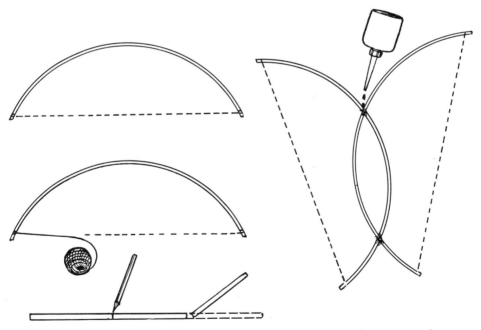

2 With a pencil mark the third stick into three equal sections. Break off one of the sections.

3 Lay the longer piece of stick up the centre of the butterfly shape, letting the same amount jut out at both top and bottom. Bind and glue the sticks together where they touch.

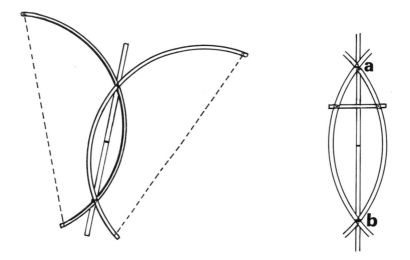

4 Push the shorter piece of stick between the centre stick and the bows half way between the top join and the pencil marking (see diagram). Bind and glue it to the bows.

5 Cover the framework with paper (see page 12).

Bridle (see page 14). Cut a piece of string a little longer than the stick down the centre. Tie it to points **a** and **b** as shown in the diagram. The curtain ring should be one third of the way down it.

Tail. This should be about twice the length of the Butterfly. Try using two or three tissue paper tassels (see page 15) instead of the usual kind of tail.

Decoration. Glue on large patches of torn tissue paper. If you let wavy edges of the paper overlap the edges of the frame, your butterfly will seem to flutter in the breeze. Experiment with overlapping pieces of tissue for subtle colour effects, and sprinkle the tissue with drops of water to make 'blotchy' spots. Paint in a black or brown body and add feelers of thin wire.

Opposite: instructions for making this flimsy-winged Insect and bright Butterfly appear on pages 54 and 30

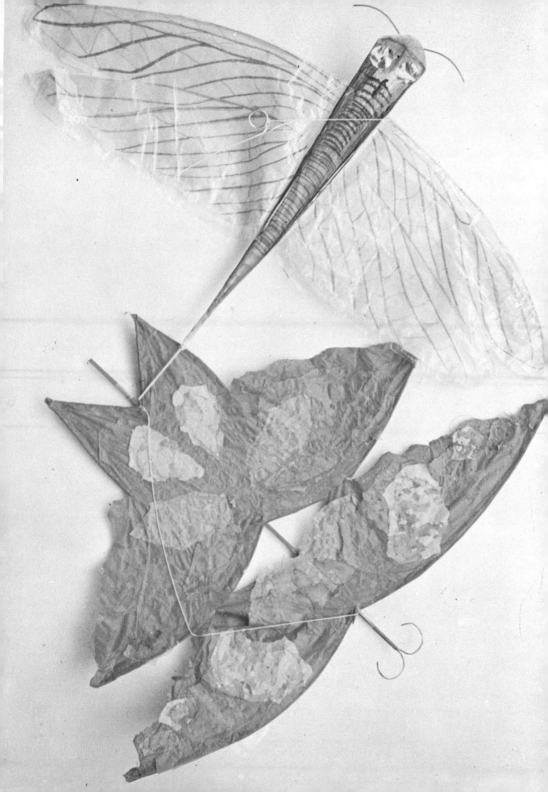

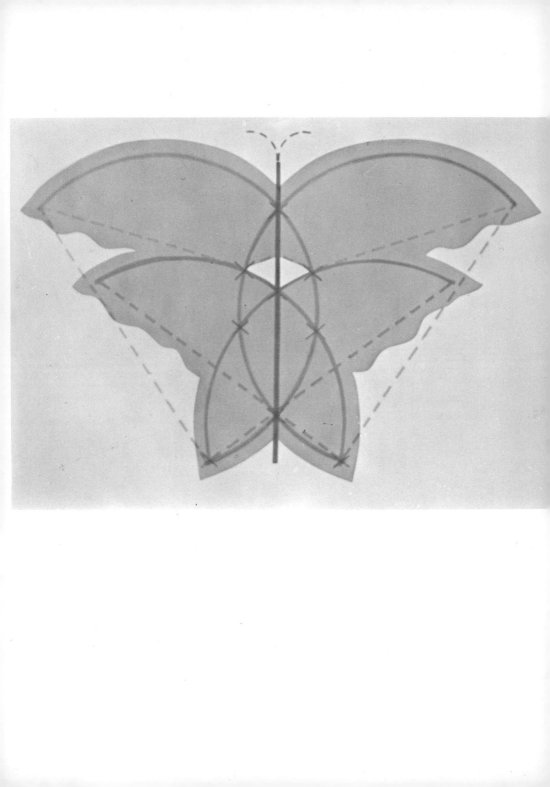

Butterfly 2 (double)

You need:
a large sheet of white paper
coloured tissue paper
1 firm stick about 50 cm (20 in.) long
2 bendy sticks about 60 cm (24 in.) long
2 bendy sticks about 90 cm (36 in.) long
string and curtain ring
glue and pencil

This is one of the most difficult kites in the book.
Practise by making a Single Butterfly first (page 30)
and then use the diagram on the facing page to help you.

1 Bow the long stick (shown in red) and the medium
sized sticks (blue) and lay them across the shorter stick
(black) to make a butterfly shape.

2 Bind and glue the sticks together wherever they cross
(points marked ×).

3 When the glue has dried, add another bow string
(green dotted line) to the longer sticks. Now remove the
first two bow strings (red dotted lines).

4 Cover the kite, leaving the lower edges of the wings
free to flutter in the breeze. Cut out the diamond shape
in the centre.

C

Carp

You need:
a sheet of paper
wire
glue
pencils and paints
scissors and glue

This kite does not fly well on its own. But try threading its towing ring onto the line when you are flying another kite and watch how quickly it skims up the line to join it.

1 Fold the paper in half. Draw the outline of the carp on the paper. Draw the mouth wider than the tail.

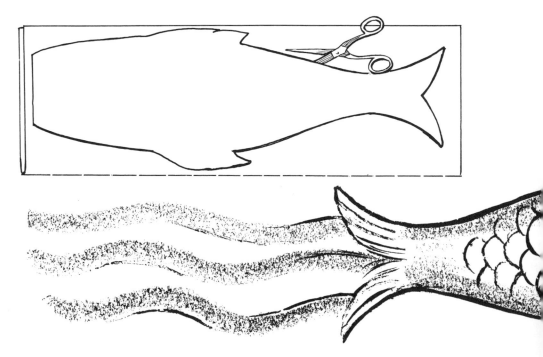

2 Cut out the shape, cutting through both layers of paper. Glue the two pieces together along the long edges. Leave the mouth and tail open.

3 Open out the mouth of the Carp and make a circle of wire the same size as the opening. Glue the wire round the mouth with a strip of paper.

Bridles. Attach four short pieces of string to the mouth of the Carp and knot them together onto a curtain ring.

Decoration. Paint eyes and scales onto your Carp and add streamers to the tail. If you use imitation Japanese paper to make this kite, you will find felt-tipped pens particularly easy and effective to work with.

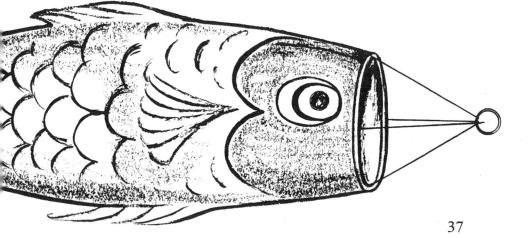

Chinaman

You need:
6 sticks the same length
paper
Polyfilla (or chewing-gum)
glue
string, curtain ring

1 Lay out three sticks to form a triangle. Join the corners with small balls of Polyfilla. (If you have no Polyfilla, use chewing-gum instead.)

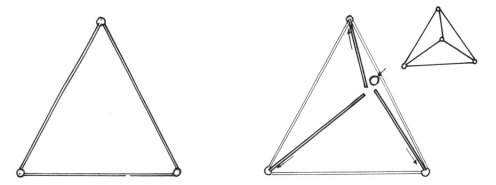

2 Stand another stick upright in each of the balls of Polyfilla. Bring the free ends of these three sticks together so that they touch. Join them by pushing onto them another small ball of Polyfilla.

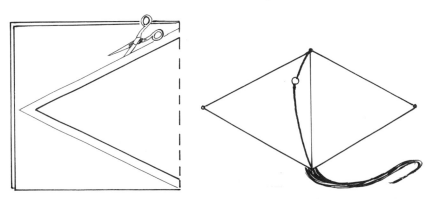

3 Fold the sheet of paper in half. Stand the frame on it, with one side of the triangular base along the fold in the paper. Cut along the other two sides of the base, making the paper shape larger than the frame on these two sides. Open out the paper shape and use it to cover two sides of the pyramid (see page 12).

Bridle (see page 14). Use a piece of string one and a half times the length of one of the sticks. Tie it to each end of the stick around which the paper is folded. Slip the curtain ring one third of the way along it.

Tail. Use a single strip of paper or cloth three times the length of one stick.

Decoration. Paint a face on the kite. Use the fold in the paper for the nose and paint one slanted eye on each side of it. Paint a moustache over the mouth and let the tail act as a beard.

Clown

You need:
2 sticks the same length
1 stick about 12 cm (5 in.)
   longer
string, curtain ring
sheet of paper
glue
paints, pencil, ruler

1 Using the pencil and
ruler, divide each stick
into four equal parts.
Using the pencil marks as
guides, lay the shorter
sticks across the other one,
as shown in the diagram.

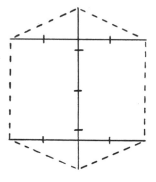

2 Bind and glue the sticks
together where they touch
(see page 10).

3 Frame the sticks with
cord or string (see page 11).

4 Cover the frame with
paper (see page 12).

5 Bow the two shorter
sticks (see page 13).

Bridle. Cut a piece of string long enough to reach from **a** to **x** and back to **a**. With the point of your pencil make a small hole in the cover each side of the stick at the two points marked **a**. Turn the kite over. Tie the ends of the string to the stick by threading them through the holes in the cover. Do not forget the curtain ring.

Cut a second piece of string to reach from **b** to **y** to **b**.

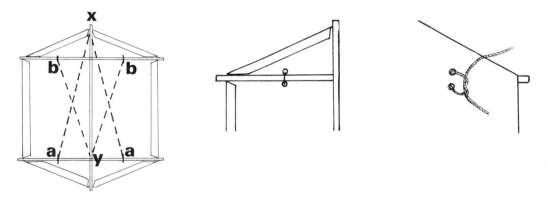

Make holes in the cover and tie the string to the points marked **b**. Slip the ring to the centre of each piece of string.

Tail. Make a tail three times the length of the kite. Tie it to the bottom of the kite.

Decoration. Use paints or cut or torn paper to make the Clown's face. If you think the shape of the kite is rather like a shield you may like to make up a coat of arms to paint on it instead.

Cutter kite

You need:
2 sticks the same length
knife
ruler, pencil
string, curtain ring
and either: a large sheet of paper
        or: a large piece of fabric, needle and thread

1 Use the ruler and pencil to divide the sticks into three equal parts. Lay the sticks across each other like this. Break off one third of one of the sticks.

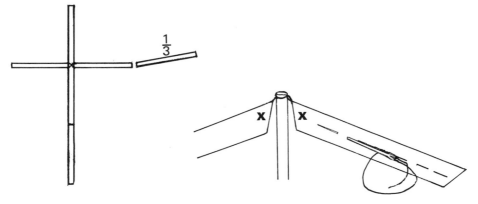

2 Bind and glue the sticks together where they touch (see page 10).

3 Make a string frame (see page 11 with the special note on cutter kites).

4 Cover the frame with paper or fabric (see page 12). If you use fabric you may still glue the edges over the frame, or you may sew it down using running stitches.

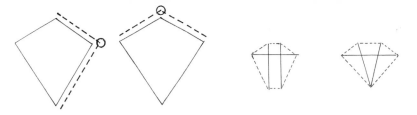

Bridles (see page 14). Cut a piece of string the length of one short and one long side of the kite. Tie it to the top and bottom. Cut a second piece the length of the two short sides of the kite and tie it to each side. Do not forget the curtain ring.

Tail (see page 15). Make a tail at least five times the length of the kite.

Variations. If you make a fabric Cutter, sew two long ribbons onto the cover at each corner at the points marked **x**. Tie each pair of ribbons together over the notch in the stick. This will help keep the cover in position and the ribbons will look pretty fluttering in the breeze.

If you wish, you can bow your kite (see page 13) to make it easier to fly. You could also add blinking eyes (see page 66).

You can also make a Cutter kite using three sticks instead of two, as shown in the two tiny diagrams at the top of the page.

Dragon

You need:
at least 12 sticks about 60 cm (24 in.) long
weaving cane
paper and glue
string and curtain ring
coloured streamers
paints or crayons

This is a difficult kite to make and an even more difficult
one to fly. But the results can be really spectacular.

The Dragon kite is made of several kites joined together.
The longer the Dragon, the more difficult it is to
manage, so try one with only six or seven sections to
begin with.

1 To make one section, mark the centre of two of the
sticks and bind and glue them together into a cross (see

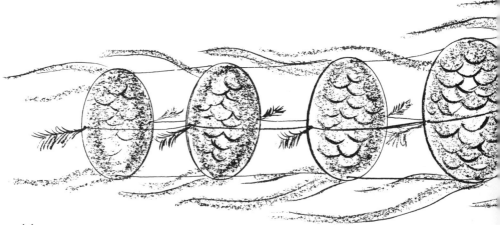

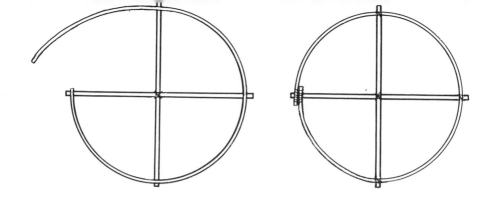

page 10). Soak the cane in water for half an hour. Bend a piece of cane into a circle round the cross. Let the ends overlap and bind and glue them together. Bind the cane to the sticks where it touches them. Cover the frame with paper (see page 12).

2 Make at least five more sections in the same way, each one a little smaller than the one before.

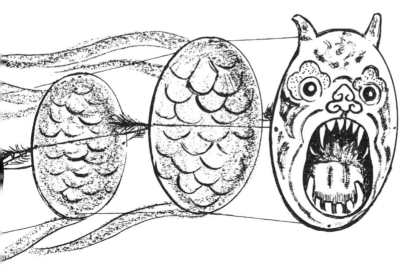

3 Make 12 large paper tassels (see page 15) and glue one to each side of each of the kite's sections.

4 Cut four pieces of string 30 cm (12 in.) long. Use them to join two kite sections together, one behind the other (see page 46). You will have to make tiny holes in the covers so that you can thread the string through them and tie the ends firmly to the sticks. Make sure you tie the top of one section to the top of the second one, the right side of one section to the right side of the next one, and so on.

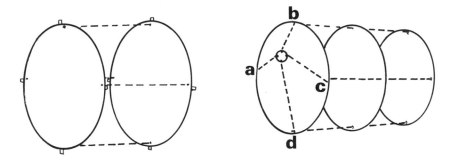

5 Join all six or seven sections one behind the other in the same way, the largest section at the front and the smallest one at the back.

Bridles (see page 14). Cut two pieces of string long enough to reach from **a** to **b** to **c**. Tie the ends of one of the pieces to points **a** and **c**, remembering to loop it through the curtain ring. Tie the ends of the second piece to points **b** and **d**. The ring should be about one third of the way along the second bridle.

Decoration. Paint the Dragon's fiery eyes and gaping jaws on the front section of the kite and paint scales on all the others. Attach coloured streamers all round the edge of all the sections.

If you prefer, you can make the Dragon of square or hexagonal sections instead of circles, as long as they are all made in exactly the same way and spaced exactly the same distance apart. The sections should graduate down in size, with the largest one at the front.

Fish

You need:
3 sticks the same length
sheet of polythene, Saran
    Wrap or similar
scraps of tissue paper
string and curtain ring
adhesive tape
glue

1 Bind and glue the sticks
together into the shape of a
star (see page 10).

2 Make a string or cord frame (see page 11).

3 Cut a polythene cover for the frame (see page 12).
Cut the cover extra wide between the top and bottom
sticks so as to give your fish a more rounded shape.

Bridles (see page 14). Use two pieces of string. One
should be long enough to reach from the two top sticks
to the centre of the kite (diagram **a**, facing page). The
other should reach from the two bottom sticks to a point
half way between the centre and the top of the kite
(diagram **b**). The curtain ring should come in the centre
of both strings.

Tail. Make one about twice the length of the kite. Tie
a loop of cord between the bottom two sticks and hang
the tail from it.

48

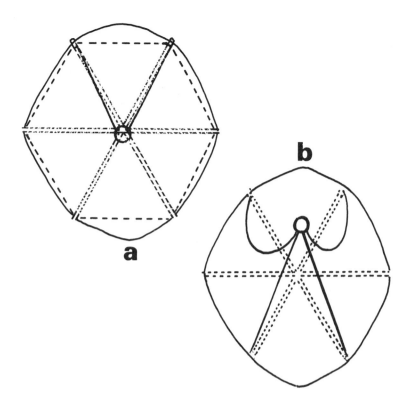

a

b

Decoration. Decorate with cut-out pieces of tissue paper glued to the cover. Some fish have stripes; some have spots. What kind of markings will yours have? Or will you give the kite a different face altogether?

Hawk

You need:
2 sticks the same length
1 stick about one third as long as the others
sheet of polythene, Saran Wrap or similar
sheet of paper
feather duster
string and curtain ring
glue and adhesive tape
pencil

1 Make this kite in the same way as the Aero-kite on page 16, but use polythene instead of paper for the cover.

2 Draw your Hawk on a sheet of paper and slip the paper under the kite. You will be able to see the outline through the cover.

3 Take the feather duster to pieces. Fill in the outline of the Hawk by gluing the feathers onto the polythene.

If you have a brightly coloured duster and not a brown one, why not make a parrot instead.

The Box kites on the facing page are surprisingly simple to make

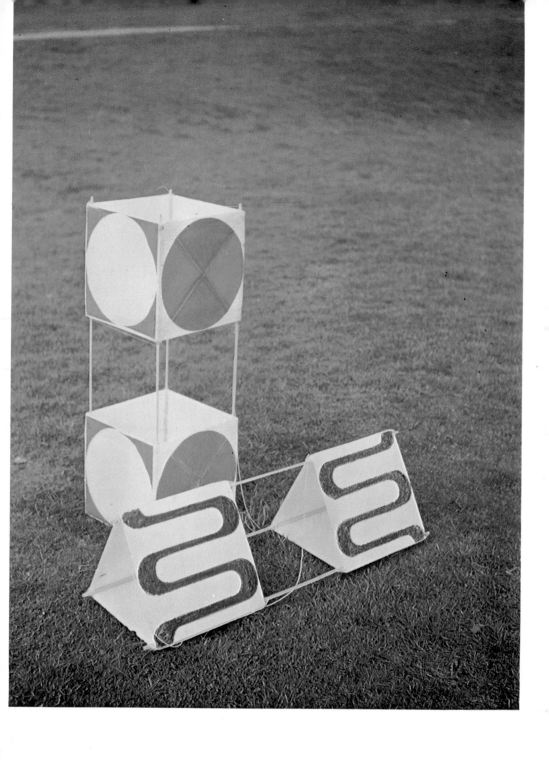

Opposite: the boy flying the Star kite is dangerously near the trees

This Hawk was made of paper in exactly the same way as the Aero-kite on pages 16–17.

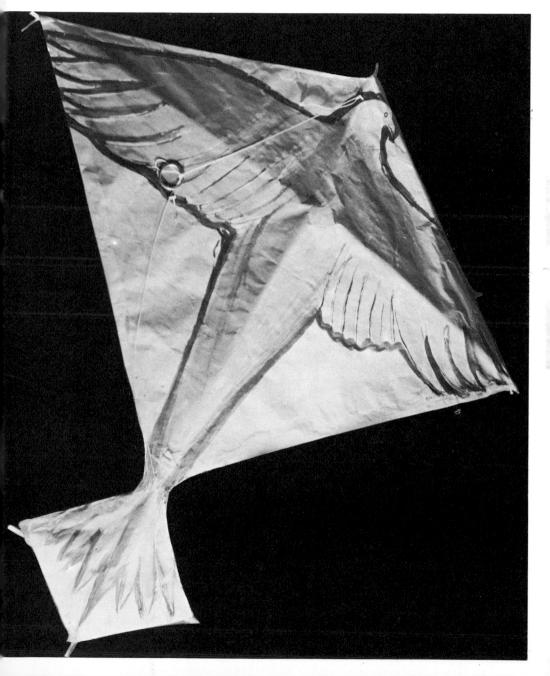

Insect

(colour photograph page 33)
You need:
3 pliable sticks, one rather longer than the other two
short piece of stick or wire (for the feelers)
sheet of paper
sheet of polythene, Saran Wrap or similar
adhesive tape, glue
string and curtain ring
paints

1 Lay the two shorter sticks together as shown in the diagram. Bind and glue them (see page 10) where they touch.

2 Bend the right-hand stick sharply at the points marked **x**. Tie and glue it to the other stick to make the head.

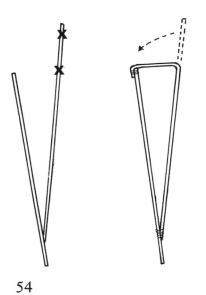

3 Cover this body section with paper (see page 12).

4 Soak the third stick in water for about half an hour. Then lay it across the others as shown. Bind and glue them where they touch.

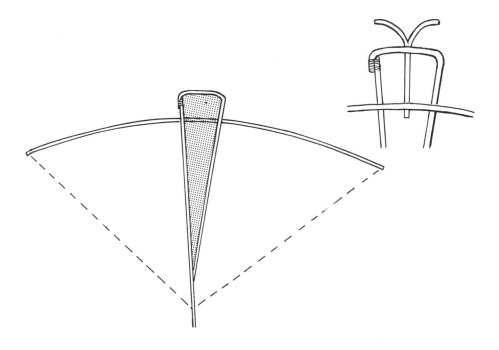

5 Tie the ends of the longer stick to the tail so that the stick is bowed. Allow the stick to dry and remove the strings. The stick should now stay bowed of its own accord.

6 Split a piece of stick half way along or bend a piece of wire to make the feelers. Bind or glue the wire or stick to the wrong side of the frame as shown.

7 Make paper wings for the Insect. Lay the framework on the sheet of paper and use the bowed stick as a guide for the top edges.

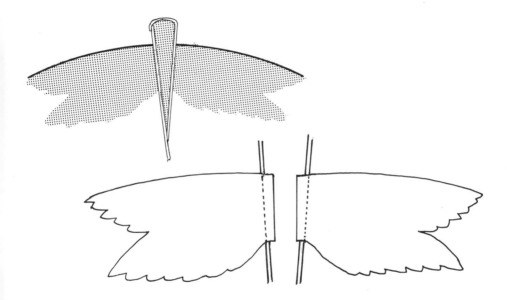

8 Allow a little extra on the inside edge of each wing as shown in the diagram.

9 Bend the top of each wing over the bowed stick and glue it down. Glue the inside edge of each wing to the under-side of the body section.

10 Paint the body and wings. Cut out two eyes of silver or gold paper and glue them on.

11 Crumple a sheet of polythene up tight and then smooth it out again. Cut some polythene wings in the same way as for the paper ones. Make them larger than the paper wings at the bottom edges.

12 Stick the polythene wings onto the paper ones with adhesive tape.

Bridles. Cut a piece of string long enough to reach from **a** to **b** and back. Tie it to the points marked **a**. Cut a second piece long enough to reach from **c** to **a**. Tie one end to point **c** and the other to the curtain ring.

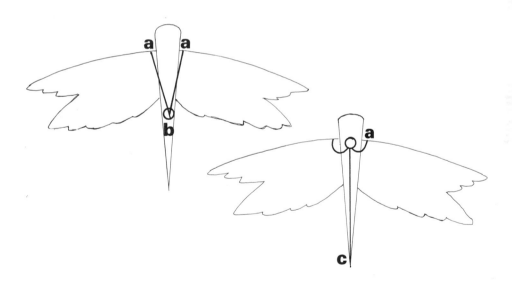

Tail. This kite needs only a very light tail and may fly without any tail at all.

Star

(photograph page 52)
You need:
4 sticks the same length
paper or foil
string and curtain ring
glue
adhesive tape

1 Mark the centre of two of the sticks. Lay them across each other, at right angles, the centre marks touching. Bind and glue them where they touch (see page 10).

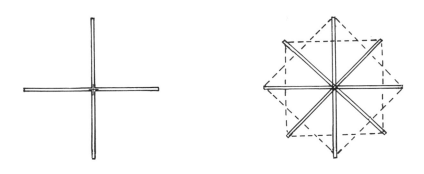

2 Frame the sticks with string (see page 11).

3 Make an identical frame with the other two sticks.

4 Lay one frame over the other so that the corners of the top one come mid way between the corners of·the bottom one. Bind and glue them together in the centre.

5 Cover the frame with paper or foil (see page 12).

Bridles (see page 14). Cut one piece of string to reach from **a** to the centre of the kite and back to **b**. Cut another to reach from **c** to **x** to **d**. Tie them to points **a**, **b**, **c** and **d**. (You will have to make small holes in the cover so as to attach the bridles from the front of the kite. This is described in the Clown section on page 39.)

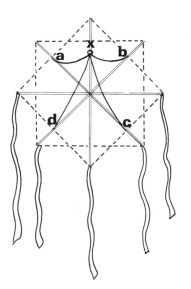

Tails. You need a tail for each of the five bottom points of the Star. Long strips of paper are best, as they tangle less easily. The middle tail should be at least three times as long as the kite. Those on each side of it should be twice the length of the kite, and those on the outside should be at least the same length as the kite.

Decoration. The Star is very effective when left plain, but you can paint a design on it if you wish.

Novelties

There are many things you can do to your kite to make it that extra bit different from everyone else's. Here are some ideas.

Attachments
Try making a 'musical' kite by fixing small whistles or bells to it. Tails or tinfoil milk bottle tops strung together will make a thin tinkly noise. If you have a very small torch, try taping it to the back of the kite so that the light shines through the cover. This is particularly effective on a Bat or Star.

Blinking eyes
A 'face' kite looks good with blinking eyes. You need a small toothpick or cocktail stick for each eye and also a small circle of stiff coloured paper. Punch two holes in each circle of paper and push a stick through them as shown in diagram **a**. Cut holes in the kite where the eyes should be, making sure they are larger than the paper circles. Fix the sticks across the holes with adhesive tape. The paper circles will spin in the wind and the eyes will seem to open and close.

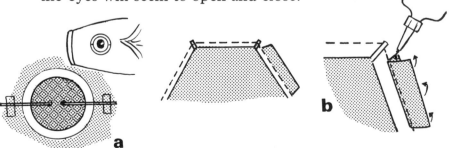

Hummers
Clowns, Cutters, Fish and Stars can all be made with hummers. Frame the kite in the usual way, then add a

second frame a little inside the first one. Cover the kite using the inner frame and leaving the outer one free. Cut some long thin strips of paper and fold and glue them lengthwise over the outer frame (diagram **b**, page 60). It is surprising how loudly these strips 'hum' in the wind.

Messages
It is easy to send a message up the line to a kite. Use a stiff circle of paper with a cut from one edge to just past the centre. If you slip it onto the line the wind will take it right up to the kite.

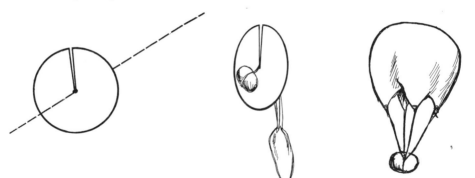

Parachutes
Make a light parachute out of a small square of thin fabric (an old handkerchief, perhaps) with a thread attached to each corner. Tie these threads to a cork or tiny pebble. To send the parachute up, slip the threads down the slit in a message disc. The cork or pebble should be right up close to the disc with the threads and fabric hanging down on the other side. Send the message up the line in the usual way and jerk the line when you want to release the parachute. It will then float down slowly to the ground.

When and where to fly your kite

Choose a day when the
breeze is steady but not
too strong. If the treetops
are bending, then the wind
is too strong for flying
kites.

Use your Carp kite as a
guide. Hold it by the
towing ring at arm's
length.

If it just hangs limp, the
breeze is too gentle for
flying any kites at all.

If it fills with air and
blows out to the side, the
breeze is right for light
and medium weight kites.

If it blows straight out to
the side, spins and tugs at
the ring, the wind is only
suitable for large, fairly
heavy kites.

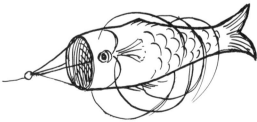

The best place for flying a kite is an open field or park where there are no trees or telegraph poles. The boy on page 52 is much too close to the trees.

If you want to fly your kite from a hill, do not go right up to the top. Stand on the windy side of the hill about 20 metres from the top. Here the wind has to rise to clear the top of the hill and will make your kite rise with it.

WARNING!

Never fly a kite with a wet line.

Never use a wire line.

Do not fly a kite anywhere near an airfield. In Britain you must be at least 5 kilometres (4 miles) away.

Do not fly your kite higher than 60 metres (200 ft.). If you do you will create real danger to aircraft and in Britain you will be breaking the law.

Equipment you need for flying your kite

To fly a kite you need:

1 *a line*
String, nylon or terylene cord, or nylon fishing line are all suitable.

2 *pair of gloves*
Always wear gloves to prevent the line from cutting into your hands.

3 *extra tail*
This is a very useful thing to have with you. You will be surprised how often your kites need a longer or heavier tail than the one you have given them.

4 *clip*
If you have more than one kite and only one line, tie a clip from a dog's lead to the end of the line so that you can switch it easily from one towing ring to another.

5 *reel*
You can use a firm cardboard tube, or an old fishing reel, or make one of these designs in wood.

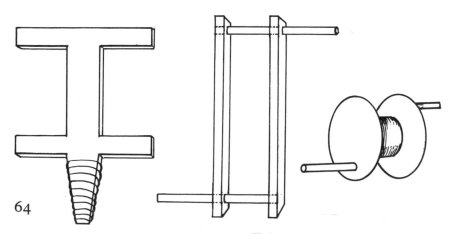

How to launch, fly and land your kite

Launching
Always stand with your back to the wind. Hold the kite by the towing ring at arm's length. The wind should simply lift it into the air, and it should not be necessary to run with the kite.

If you have a helper ask him to stand a little way in front of you, holding the kite tilted into the breeze. He should wait until the wind lifts the kite out of his hands and should never throw it into the air.

If you have an extra large Box kite, stand it on the ground in front of you, the bridle towards the wind. Pull the line gently to tilt the kite. The wind should now lift it off the ground.

Flying
Do not let the line out too quickly once the kite is off the ground.

Help the kite to rise by pulling on the line. To do this, grip the line at arm's length. Bend your arm up and right back at the elbow, still gripping the line. Straighten your arm again slowly, at the same time letting the line slip through your fingers. Grip the line again and continue pulling and releasing it in this way until the kite is high enough in the sky.

If the kite slips slowly to the left, run across the breeze to the left. If it slips to the right, then run to the right.

If the kite dives suddenly to one side, quickly let out more line.

Adjusting

A flat kite should lean forward into the wind and fly at an angle of about 45°.

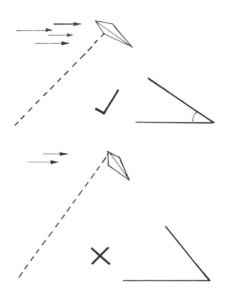

If your kite will not rise, perhaps it is flying too vertically. Move the towing ring nearer the top of the kite.

If your kite flutters, dips and thrashes about, perhaps it is flying too flat to the wind. Move the towing ring nearer the middle of the kite.

If your kite falls to the left, try moving the towing ring a little to the right. If it slips to the right, move the ring a little to the left.

If your kite dives, or spins, or loops the loop you must add a longer or heavier tail.

If the kite does not rise and the tail hangs down instead of streaming out behind, then you must shorten the tail.

Landing

Make sure there is no-one standing in front of you before you land your kite. Kites often crash when they come in low.

In a light breeze, simply wind in the line. In a stronger breeze, walk towards the kite as you wind in the line.

If you have a helper, ask him to hold the reel while you put your hand over the line and walk towards the kite, letting the line slip through your fingers. This will bring the kite down gradually.

Box kites sometimes drop suddenly when they are being reeled in. If your helper is *very* careful he could try to catch it before it touches the ground.

Index